Would You
Rather?
Summer
EDITION

Would You Rather?

Summer
EDITION

Laugh-Out-Loud Game
for Camping, Road Trips,
and Vacation Travel

LINDSEY DALY

Z KIDS · NEW YORK

For Kelly, thank you for being an amazing
friend and my unofficial publicist.

Contents

INTRODUCTION 8
RULES OF THE GAME 10

ROUND
1
Road Trip!
13

ROUND
2
Camping Qs
27

ROUND
3
Outdoor Adventure
41

ROUND
4
Go Wild!
55

ROUND

5

Summer Camp

69

ROUND

6

Armchair Traveler

83

ROUND

7

Home Base

97

ROUND

8

Rainy-Day Fun

111

WINNER'S CERTIFICATE 125

Introduction

There are a million fun ways to enjoy summer: traveling to a new destination for vacation, going to camp, practicing your favorite sport, spending days at the pool with friends—the list goes on and on! But just because school is out for the summer doesn't mean you should stop exercising your brain. That's where *Would You Rather? Summer Edition* comes in. It's the perfect way to practice your critical-thinking skills while laughing with friends using 160+ questions about everyone's favorite season.

Spruce up any sleepover, long drive, or camping trip by learning the inner workings of your friends' minds. "Would You Rather?" questions are excellent conversation starters and are designed to invite funny, thoughtful, and creative discussions. The questions are for kids ages 8–12 but they're sure to entertain the whole family. You never know what fascinating details you might learn about what and how other people think!

Would You Rather? Summer Edition can be played as a game, with winners for individual questions, chapters, and the entire book, based on humor, logic, and overall creativity. Whether you play it as a game or not, these funny and thought-provoking summer scenarios will stretch your imagination and put your mind to the test. Get ready to show off your critical-thinking skills, interact with friends and family, and most importantly, have fun!

Rules of
the Game

~~~~~~

Get a group of friends or family members together for a game of wits and creativity. The more the merrier!

* The game is played in eight rounds, with twenty questions in each round.

* Players rotate the responsibility of being the "judge" and read the question aloud to the group.

* Players will then respond with an explanation and take turns sharing their answers.

* The judge of that round will choose the best answer based on humor, creativity, or logic. Write the winner's name in the space provided below the question and assign them one point. If only two people are playing, the judge (the player reading the question) assigns 1 to 5 points for the answer (5 being the best answer) and records it with the

other player's name in the space provided below the question.

* When all players complete the round, tally up the points to determine the winner for that round.

* In the event of a tie at the end of a round, the two players who are tied will answer the tiebreaker question. All remaining players will vote on the best answer. If only two people are playing, whoever makes the other player laugh wins.

* When all players complete the book, the winner of the most rounds is the champion!

ROUND

1

Road Trip!

Would you rather
sit in the back seat with
people and luggage
or
in the front seat without
any leg room?

WINNER: POINTS:

Would you rather
ride in a car with someone
who keeps sneezing
or
coughing?

WINNER: POINTS:

Would you rather
go on a road trip without
any snacks
or
drinks?

WINNER: POINTS:

Would you rather
tour the country in an
RV with your family
or
in a minivan with your
best friend?

WINNER: POINTS:

Would you rather
stop at every national park
or
every major city?

WINNER: POINTS:

Would you rather
drive with someone who smells bad
or
never stops talking?

WINNER: POINTS:

Would you rather
road trip with no air-conditioning
or
windows you can't see out of?

WINNER: POINTS:

Would you rather
drive a convertible through a
thunderstorm
or
a dust storm?

WINNER: POINTS:

Would you rather
be strapped to the roof of a car
or
ride in the trunk?

WINNER: POINTS:

Would you rather
drive through the night
on no sleep
or
drive during the day
in heavy traffic?

WINNER: POINTS:

Would you rather
listen to an audiobook
that you don't like
or
a podcast that you
find boring?

WINNER: POINTS:

Would you rather
forget to pack your underwear
or
your phone charger?

WINNER: POINTS:

Would you rather

be stuck in the car with someone
who sings off-key

or

a staticky radio?

WINNER: POINTS:

Would you rather

eat all your snacks in the first
hour of a long road trip

or

have your phone battery die?

WINNER: POINTS:

Would you rather
get carsick halfway through your trip
or
constantly have a runny nose
and no tissues?

WINNER: POINTS:

Would you rather
get stuck behind a bicycle race
or
a horse and carriage?

WINNER: POINTS:

Would you rather
run out of gas on a
deserted back road
or
in the middle of a
busy highway?

WINNER: POINTS:

Would you rather
listen to your favorite song on
repeat for the whole trip
or
a variety of songs you've
never heard before?

WINNER: POINTS:

Would you rather

spend a 20-hour road trip listening
to only classical music
or
children's songs?

WINNER: POINTS:

Would you rather

get lost in a scenic small town
or
a bustling city?

WINNER: POINTS:

Would you rather

take a road trip on a school bus

or

in an eighteen-wheeler truck?

WINNER: POINTS:

WINNER: _____

TOTAL POINTS: _____

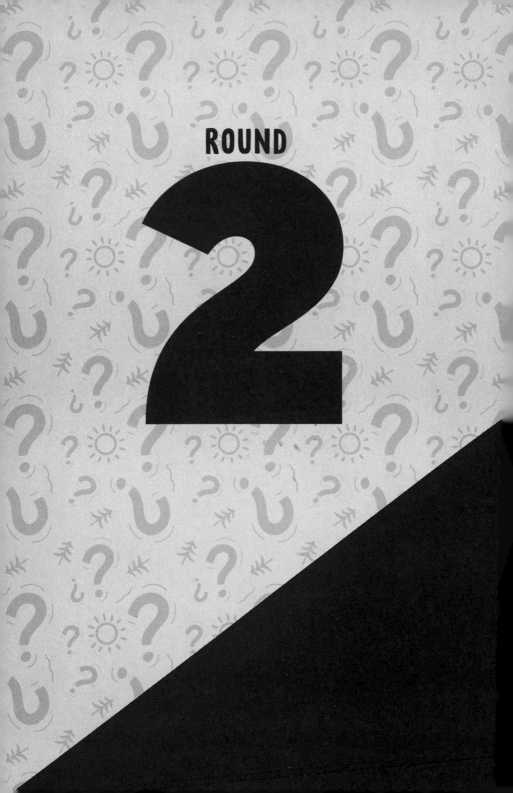

ROUND

2

Camping Qs

Would you rather
start a campfire in the rain
or
lose a paddle canoeing?

WINNER: POINTS:

Would you rather
have a bear steal all your food
or
your cell phone?

WINNER: POINTS:

Would you rather
be attacked by a swarm
of mosquitos
or
an extremely determined wasp?

WINNER: POINTS:

Would you rather
go on a weeklong camping trip
without a change of clothes
or
a water bottle?

WINNER: POINTS:

Would you rather
eat a s'more that fell in the dirt
or
has a dead bug in it?

WINNER: POINTS:

Would you rather
sleep alone in a tent
in the woods
or
camp with a friend who
left the tent at home?

WINNER: POINTS:

Would you rather
find a snake in your tent
or
a colony of ants?

WINNER: POINTS:

Would you rather
go glamping at a camp resort
or
explore a national park in an RV?

WINNER: POINTS:

Would you rather

stay at a haunted campground

or

one known for lots of bears?

WINNER: POINTS:

Would you rather

share ghost stories around the campfire at night

or

play Manhunt in the woods?

WINNER: POINTS:

Would you rather
float down a river in a tube
or
go white water rafting?

WINNER: POINTS:

Would you rather
forget your sleeping bag
or
the materials you need
to start a campfire?

WINNER: POINTS:

Would you rather
spend the night stranded
on a lake in a leaky canoe
or
on a pool float?

WINNER: POINTS:

Would you rather
eat nothing but burnt
hot dogs for a week
or
canned beans?

WINNER: POINTS:

Would you rather

sleep in a hammock on a windy night

or

in a sleeping bag on damp ground?

WINNER: POINTS:

Would you rather

get campfire smoke in your eyes

or

swallow a mouthful of bug spray?

WINNER: POINTS:

Would you rather
camp for a week without showering
or
bathe in an outdoor shower
covered in bugs?

WINNER: POINTS:

Would you rather
forget to pack your sunscreen
or
your flashlight?

WINNER: POINTS:

Would you rather
hear bears growling in
the woods at night
or
coyotes howling?

WINNER: POINTS:

Would you rather
camp on the beach
or
in the mountains?

WINNER: POINTS:

Would you rather

discover a compass if you were
lost in the wilderness

or

a first aid kit?

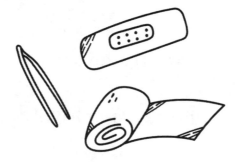

WINNER: POINTS:

WINNER

ROUND 2

WINNER: _____

TOTAL POINTS: _____

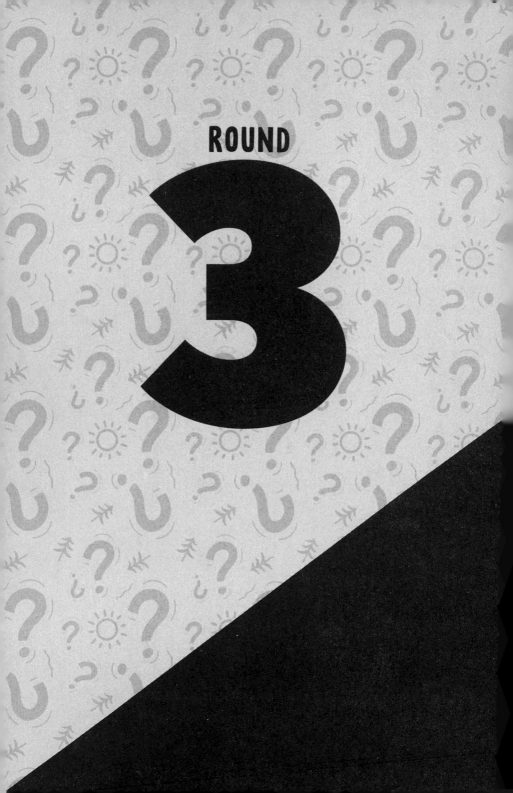

ROUND

3

Outdoor Adventure

Would you rather
go zip-lining over an active volcano
or
shark-infested waters?

WINNER: POINTS:

Would you rather
go bird-watching
or
fly-fishing?

WINNER: POINTS:

Would you rather
fall off a white water raft
or
a deep-sea fishing boat?

WINNER: POINTS:

Would you rather
hike up a mountain
wearing flip-flops
or
through the woods
with bare feet?

WINNER: POINTS:

Would you rather

climb a mountain during a heat wave

or

paraglide in a thunderstorm?

WINNER: POINTS:

Would you rather

sail across the ocean on a boat with no beds

or

no motor?

WINNER: POINTS:

Would you rather
swim with stingrays
or
piranhas?

WINNER: POINTS:

Would you rather
race someone on a horse
or
a motorcycle?

WINNER: POINTS:

Would you rather
run a marathon on the windiest
day of the summer
or
the most humid?

WINNER: POINTS:

Would you rather
ride an ATV through a desert
or
parasail along a beach?

WINNER: POINTS:

Would you rather
surf the largest wave
ever recorded
or
skateboard down the world's
steepest half-pipe?

WINNER: POINTS:

Would you rather
go rock climbing without a harness
or
zip-lining?

WINNER: POINTS:

Would you rather
surf without taking any lessons
or
kayak down a waterfall?

WINNER: POINTS:

Would you rather
ride two miles on a unicycle
or
a Hoverboard?

WINNER: POINTS:

Would you rather
go cliff diving
or
bungee jumping off a bridge?

WINNER: POINTS:

Would you rather
ride down a hill on a bicycle
with broken brakes
or
Rollerblades?

WINNER: POINTS:

Would you rather
swim across a lake alone at night
or
go on a hike?

WINNER: POINTS:

Would you rather
drop your phone into a hot spring
or
the Grand Canyon?

WINNER: POINTS:

Would you rather
use a sneaker as a kayak paddle
or
a pasta strainer?

WINNER: POINTS:

Would you rather
go spear fishing off the coast
or
deep-sea fishing in the
middle of the ocean?

WINNER: POINTS:

Would you rather

hike on the hottest day of summer

or

the coldest day of winter?

WINNER: POINTS:

WINNER:

TOTAL POINTS:

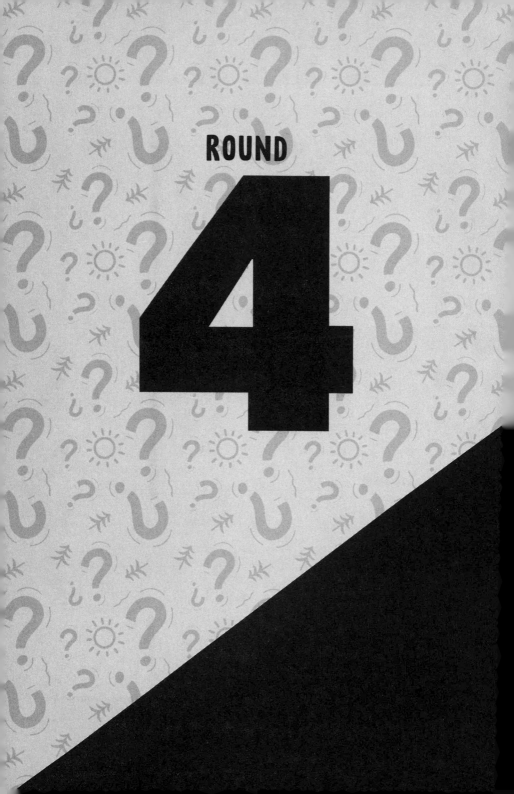

ROUND
4

Go Wild!

Would you rather
feed a skunk
or
a bear?

WINNER: POINTS:

Would you rather
raise a baby owl
or
a chimpanzee?

WINNER: POINTS:

Would you rather
spend two weeks at a lake house
or
one week in a beach house?

WINNER: POINTS:

Would you rather
encounter a moose in the woods
or
a bobcat?

WINNER: POINTS:

Would you rather
keep a fox as a pet
or
an otter?

WINNER: POINTS:

Would you rather
live in a house in the
middle of the woods
or
on a remote island?

WINNER: POINTS:

Would you rather
be a tree for a day
or
a flower?

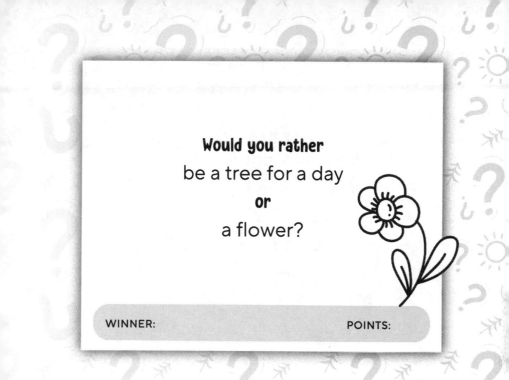

WINNER: POINTS:

Would you rather
live in a desert
or
a rain forest?

WINNER: POINTS:

Would you rather
be a photographer for
National Geographic
or
a meteorologist on TV?

WINNER: POINTS:

Would you rather
drink salt water
or
lake water?

WINNER: POINTS:

Would you rather
sleep in a swamp
or
a sewer?

WINNER: POINTS:

Would you rather
have to survive in the wilderness
for a reality show
or
participate in an athletic
competition?

WINNER: POINTS:

Would you rather
be covered in mosquito bites
or
poison ivy?

WINNER: POINTS:

Would you rather
have to hunt for your food
or
find your own source of water?

WINNER: POINTS:

Would you rather
eat a handful of wild berries
or
mushrooms?

WINNER: POINTS:

Would you rather
be bitten by a spider
or
a snake?

WINNER: POINTS:

Would you rather
discover a cave with
ancient wall paintings
or
an artifact from a historic event?

WINNER: POINTS:

Would you rather
cuddle with a koala
or
a sloth?

WINNER: POINTS:

Would you rather
everything smelled like
a skunk for a month
or
horse manure?

WINNER: POINTS:

Would you rather
raise farm animals
or
exotic animals?

WINNER: POINTS:

Would you rather
experience all four
seasons each year
or
only your favorite one?

WINNER: POINTS:

WINNER

ROUND 4

WINNER:

TOTAL POINTS:

ROUND

5

Summer Camp

Would you rather
take archery lessons
or
a class on outdoor survival skills?

WINNER: POINTS:

Would you rather
share a bunk with someone
who snores loudly
or
never showers?

WINNER: POINTS:

Would you rather
sleep in a tent with access
to a bathroom
or
a cabin that has a porta-potty?

WINNER: POINTS:

Would you rather
have to clean cabins
or
cook camp food?

WINNER: POINTS:

Would you rather
attend a performing
arts camp
or
a science camp?

WINNER: POINTS:

Would you rather
be a camp counselor
or
a lifeguard?

WINNER: POINTS:

Would you rather
go sailing with someone
terrified of water
or
horseback riding on
an anxious horse?

WINNER: POINTS:

Would you rather
make bottle rockets
or
catapult cannons?

WINNER: POINTS:

Would you rather
go foraging
in the woods
or
build your own
shelter?

WINNER: POINTS:

Would you rather
sleep on the top bunk
or
the bottom bunk?

WINNER: POINTS:

Would you rather
bunk with your best friend
and nine strangers
or
no best friend and nine pals?

WINNER: POINTS:

Would you rather
accidentally get locked in an
outhouse for a night
or
be lost in the woods?

WINNER: POINTS:

Would you rather
make one phone call a day
or
receive unlimited letters?

WINNER: POINTS:

Would you rather
sing songs around the campfire
or
tell scary stories?

WINNER: POINTS:

Would you rather
be assigned the cabin
closest to the lake
or
the dining hall?

WINNER: POINTS:

Would you rather
go to a summer camp alone
or
with a frenemy?

WINNER: POINTS:

Would you rather
sneak a phone into camp
or
a gaming system?

WINNER: POINTS:

Would you rather
have a camp counselor
who is fun but lazy
or
strict but plans great activities?

WINNER: POINTS:

Would you rather
walk through the woods
alone at night
or
sleep in your bunk by yourself?

WINNER: POINTS:

Would you rather
have your parents work at
your summer camp
or
your older sibling be your
camp counselor?

WINNER: POINTS:

Would you rather
hike to the highest point in
camp with a sprained ankle
or
go rock climbing with
a broken finger?

WINNER: POINTS:

WINNER

WINNER: _____

TOTAL POINTS: _____

ROUND

6

Armchair Traveler

Would you rather
be the first visitor at a new resort
or
on a cruise ship's maiden voyage?

WINNER: POINTS:

Would you rather
go whale watching
or
swim with dolphins?

WINNER: POINTS:

Would you rather
review hotels
or
film a travel show?

WINNER: POINTS:

Would you rather
visit a new place for five days
or
a place you've already
been for ten days?

WINNER: POINTS:

Would you rather
be the host of a docuseries
about exotic animals
or
historical landmarks?

WINNER: POINTS:

Would you rather
use virtual reality to ride the world's
best roller coasters
or
explore the depths of the ocean?

WINNER: POINTS:

Would you rather
go island-hopping on a yacht
or
fly around the world in a private jet?

WINNER: POINTS:

Would you rather
host a podcast about exotic
travel destinations
or
travel nightmares?

WINNER: POINTS:

Would you rather
travel alone
or
with a former friend?

WINNER: POINTS:

Would you rather
have your seatmate on a plane
throw up mid-flight
or
fall asleep and drool
on your shoulder?

WINNER: POINTS:

Would you rather
host a YouTube channel
about hiking
or
geocaching?

WINNER: POINTS:

Would you rather
swim with tropical fish
or
fly with exotic birds?

WINNER: POINTS:

Would you rather
visit ten different European
countries by train
or
boat?

WINNER: POINTS:

Would you rather
visit every amusement
park in the country
or
the top of the tallest
building in each state?

WINNER: POINTS:

Would you rather
explore ancient ruins
or
relax on the beach?

WINNER: POINTS:

Would you rather
tour a beautiful city
via hot-air balloon
or
helicopter?

WINNER: POINTS:

Would you rather
spend a week at Giraffe Manor
in Kenya
or
on an alpaca farm in France?

WINNER: POINTS:

Would you rather
miss your flight
or
sit in the plane on the runway for
five hours before taking off?

WINNER: POINTS:

Would you rather
take a boat tour of glaciers
or
crystal caves?

WINNER: POINTS:

Would you rather
ride a donkey through
the Swiss Alps
or
a camel in the desert?

WINNER: POINTS:

TIEBREAKER

Would you rather
have the airline lose
your luggage
or
get airsick on the way
to your destination?

WINNER: POINTS:

WINNER

ROUND
6

WINNER: _____

TOTAL POINTS: _____

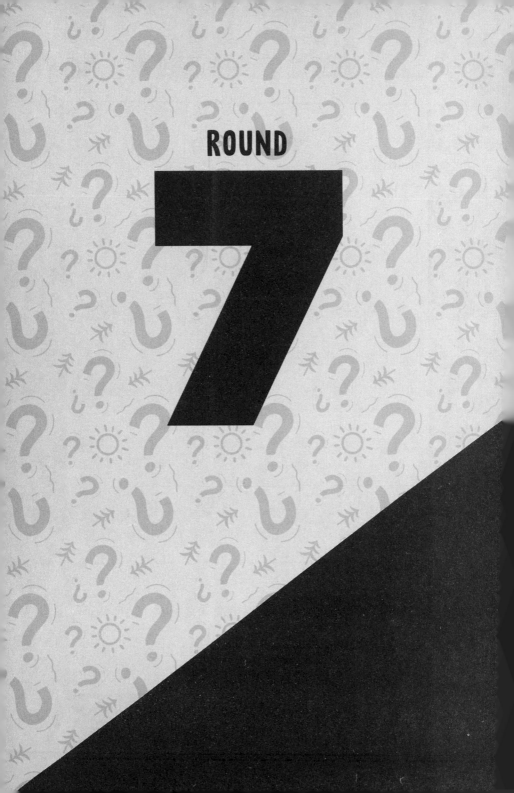

ROUND

7

Home Base

Would you rather
play a game of Manhunt with all
the kids in your neighborhood
or
kickball?

WINNER: POINTS:

Would you rather
have a miniature golf
coursein your backyard
or
a sand volleyball court?

WINNER: POINTS:

Would you rather
drop your phone into the
lion habitat at the zoo
or
the gorilla enclosure?

WINNER: POINTS:

Would you rather
fall off your bike into a pond
or
a pricker bush?

WINNER: POINTS:

Would you rather
build a tree house in
your backyard
or
a zip line?

WINNER: POINTS:

Would you rather
host a campout for your
friends in your backyard
or
a pool party?

WINNER: POINTS:

Would you rather
play Capture the Flag with your
friends against your teachers
or
your friends' parents?

WINNER: POINTS:

Would you rather
attend a bonfire
or
a block party?

WINNER: POINTS:

Would you rather
try to catch fish using a bucket
or
a pointy stick?

WINNER: POINTS:

Would you rather
get paid to mow your
neighbor's lawn
or
clean out their pool?

WINNER: POINTS:

Would you rather
complete your summer
reading assignment during
the first week of summer
or
the last week?

WINNER: POINTS:

Would you rather
spend an entire summer
without air-conditioning
or
video games?

WINNER: POINTS:

Would you rather
discover that none of your friends
will be home for the summer
or
break your leg on the first
day of vacation?

WINNER: POINTS:

Would you rather
spend the summer volunteering
with young children
or
the elderly?

WINNER: POINTS:

Would you rather
be banned from using
technology all summer
or
playing outside?

WINNER: POINTS:

Would you rather
run a lemonade stand
in your neighborhood
or
a pet-sitting business?

WINNER: POINTS:

Would you rather
attend summer school
for three weeks
or
go to work every day with
one of your parents?

WINNER: POINTS:

Would you rather
set up a movie projector
in your yard
or
a giant telescope?

WINNER: POINTS:

Would you rather
ride around town on
an electric scooter
or
a Segway?

WINNER: POINTS:

Would you rather
have your bike stolen
or
be accused of taking
someone else's?

WINNER: POINTS:

Would you rather
be banned from eating
junk food all summer
or
playing video games?

WINNER: POINTS:

WINNER

ROUND 7

WINNER: _____

TOTAL POINTS: _____

ROUND

8

Rainy-Day Fun

Would you rather
write and perform a play
with your friends
or
binge-watch your favorite
TV show?

WINNER: POINTS:

Would you rather
have a bake-off competition
with your family
or
a board game tournament?

WINNER: POINTS:

Would you rather
complete a 1,000-piece puzzle
or
an entire book of sudoku?

WINNER: _____ POINTS: _____

Would you rather
spend the day watching
your favorite movies
or
home videos of you as a baby?

WINNER: _____ POINTS: _____

Would you rather
redecorate your bedroom
or
choose the color of every
room in your home?

WINNER: POINTS:

Would you rather
have a sleepover with a
friend who sleepwalks
or
plays pranks on you
when you're asleep?

WINNER: POINTS:

Would you rather
compete in an indoor
scavenger hunt
or
complete an obstacle course?

WINNER: POINTS:

Would you rather
make a homemade
volcano
or
slime?

WINNER: POINTS:

Would you rather
build a fort using
only empty boxes
or
bedsheets?

WINNER: POINTS:

Would you rather
put together a time capsule
or
make a collage out of
your favorite photos?

WINNER: POINTS:

Would you rather
wear ridiculous clothes
in a fashion show
or
choreograph a new dance?

WINNER: POINTS:

Would you rather
create your own board game
or
code a new video game?

WINNER: POINTS:

Would you rather
drink water from a puddle
or
that drips off your roof
when it's raining?

WINNER: POINTS:

Would you rather
be stuck inside with your
family during a storm
or
be home alone?

WINNER: POINTS:

Would you rather
make up a language with
your best friend
or
a secret handshake?

WINNER: POINTS:

Would you rather
pretend that the floor is
lava for the whole day
or
try to navigate your
house in the dark?

WINNER: POINTS:

Would you rather

get locked out of your house
during a thunderstorm

or

leave your iPad outside?

WINNER: POINTS:

Would you rather

be stuck inside with someone
playing a violin badly

or

a howling dog?

WINNER: POINTS:

Would you rather
have your bedroom flooded
or
lose electricity for two days?

WINNER: POINTS:

Would you rather
be dared to take a bite out of
a piece of sidewalk chalk
or
a glue stick?

WINNER: POINTS:

Would you rather
learn how to make ice cream
or
sew?

WINNER: POINTS:

WINNER: _____

TOTAL POINTS: _____

This certificate
is awarded to

_____

for answers that are more fun
than summer vacation and
brighter than the sun!

Summer may not be endless, but
your creativity and wit sure are!

CONGRATULATIONS!

About the Author

 **Lindsey Daly** grew up in Andover, New Jersey. She graduated from Ramapo College of New Jersey with a BA in history and a certification in secondary education. Lindsey is a middle school social studies teacher and the author of the best-selling Would You Rather? series. She lives with her dog, Teddy, in New Jersey.

Parents, for more information about Lindsey and her books, follow her online:

 @lindseydalybooks

 @LindseyDaly10

Hi, Parents and caregivers,

We hope your child enjoyed *Would You Rather? Summer Edition*. If you have any questions or concerns about this book, or have received a damaged copy, please contact customerservice@penguinrandomhouse.com. We're here and happy to help. Also, please consider writing a review on your favorite retailer's website to let others know what you and your child thought of the book!

Sincerely,
The Zeitgeist Team